I0813146

Desserts from Around the World

FROZEN DESSERTS FROM AROUND THE WORLD

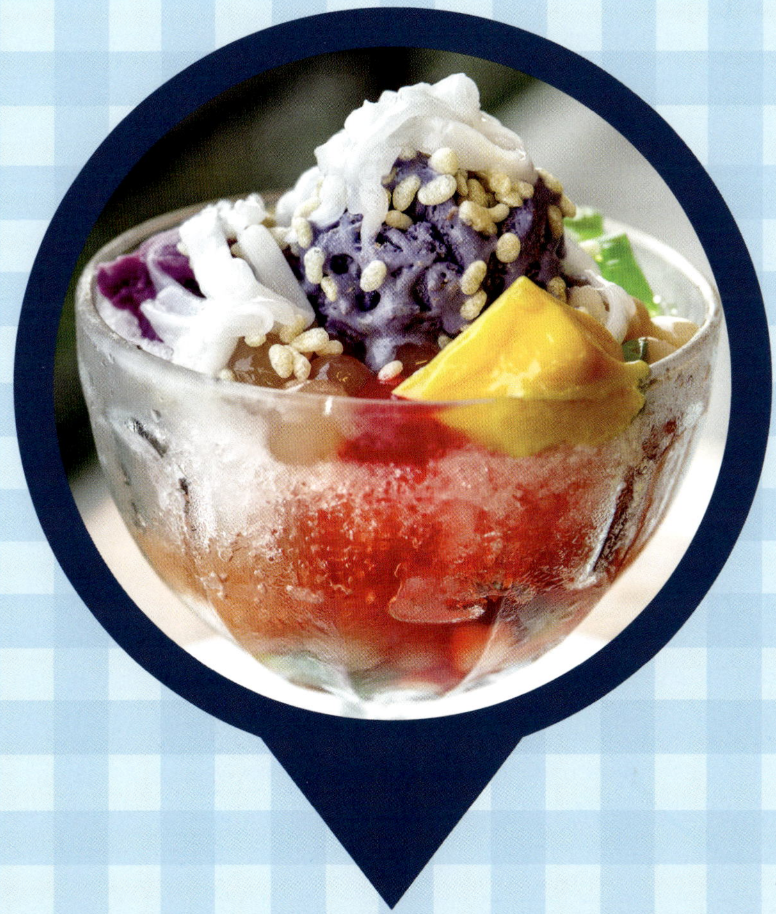

by Grace Hansen

WELCOME TO DiscoverRoo!

This book is filled with videos, puzzles, games, and more! Scan the QR codes* while you read, or visit the website below to make this book pop.

popbooksonline.com/frozen

abdobooks.com

Published by Pop!, a division of ABDO, PO Box 398166, Minneapolis, Minnesota 55439.

Printed in the United States of America, North Mankato, Minnesota.

102024
012025

Cover Photo: Shutterstock Images
Interior Photos: Shutterstock Images, Getty Images
Editor: Elizabeth Andrews
Series Designer: Laura Graphenteen

Library of Congress Control Number: 2024938605

Publisher's Cataloging-in-Publication Data

Names: Hansen, Grace, author.

Title: Frozen desserts from around the world / by Grace Hansen

Description: Minneapolis, Minnesota : Pop!, 2025 | Series: Desserts from around the world | Includes online resources and index

Identifiers: ISBN 9781098247133 (lib. bdg.) | ISBN 9781098247690 (ebook)

Subjects: LCSH: Baking--Juvenile literature. | Desserts--Juvenile literature. | Baked products--Juvenile literature. | Frozen desserts--Juvenile literature. | Frozen baked products--Juvenile literature. | Cookery--Juvenile literature.

Classification: DDC 641.862--dc23

*Scanning QR codes requires a web-enabled smart device with a QR code reader app and a camera.

TABLE OF CONTENTS

CHAPTER 1

THE HISTORY OF DESSERT

Desserts can be traced back to ancient times. The Mesopotamians had a fruitcake-like recipe. The Ancient Egyptians sweetened round, flat breads with dates and honey and cooked them over hot stones.

WATCH A VIDEO HERE!

Much of what we know about the Ancient Egyptians comes from wall paintings in temples and tombs.

The shape celebrated the sun and moon. The Ancient Romans enjoyed simple sweet treats such as fruits, honey cakes, and fruit tarts.

This English oil painting from 1867 shows a first birthday celebration with cake and a candle.

In the 7th century, Persia (now Iran) was one of the first to harvest sugar cane and make cake-like cookies. In the 1500s, sugar became more affordable and widely available. In 1596, a cookbook was published for the growing middle classes in England. In it was a recipe for Fine Cakes. Later, Europeans made it more common to serve dessert, especially cake, for special occasions such as weddings.

Between 800 and 900, the Persians brought sugar cane to Southern Europe.

To this day, desserts help people around the world start the day, complete a meal, and celebrate important **milestones** and holidays. Let's go around the world and learn about frozen desserts from different places and **cultures**!

Almond cake, such as the one in this Ancient Roman mosaic, would have required a great amount of effort to prepare.

Mochi has long been enjoyed in Japan to celebrate the New Year. It was said to harden the teeth and therefore extend life.

CHAPTER 2

FROZEN DESSERTS FROM EUROPE

In the 16th century, Italians adopted the **Turkish Empire's** tradition of putting ice into fruit drinks. It was then that they began to perfect modern Sorbet and Gelato. Italian Giovanni Biasolo first introduced Gelato to the United States in 1770. Around the same time, ice cream was becoming popular. Gelato and

LEARN MORE HERE!

Gelato is kept at a warmer temperature than ice cream. This helps give Gelato its velvety texture.

ice cream differ in their butterfat and sugar content, **churning** technique, and storage temperature. Many agree that the thickness of Gelato makes it more flavorful than ice cream.

Granita is served with brioche pastries in the morning.

Italy is famous for other frozen desserts too, including Granita, Affogato, and Tartufo di Pizzo. Granita is a grainier version of Sorbet, yet just as refreshing. Affogato combines two of Italy's favorite things: vanilla Gelato and warm espresso. Tartufo di Pizzo uses two or more flavors of Gelato rolled in ball with a delightful surprise in the center!

SUPER COOL!

Ancient Chinese, Japanese, Greeks, Romans, and Egyptians all put ice in their food and drinks. Despite living in the desert, the Ancient Egyptians found a way to make their own ice by putting water in clay pots to sit overnight. Quick **evaporation** and cooler temperatures froze the water.

Sorbet is a frozen dessert made from ice, fruit, and sugar.

CHAPTER 3

FROZEN DESSERTS FROM THE AMERICAS

Summers in the Dominican Republic can be very warm. Luckily, locals often enjoy Helado de Potecito, Spanish for "Ice Cream in a Pot." The refreshing treat is made by simply freezing fruit juice in small glass jars. Some traditional recipes call for just two ingredients, such as mango **puree** mixed with strawberries.

EXPLORE LINKS HERE!

No sugar is added to Helado de Potecito.

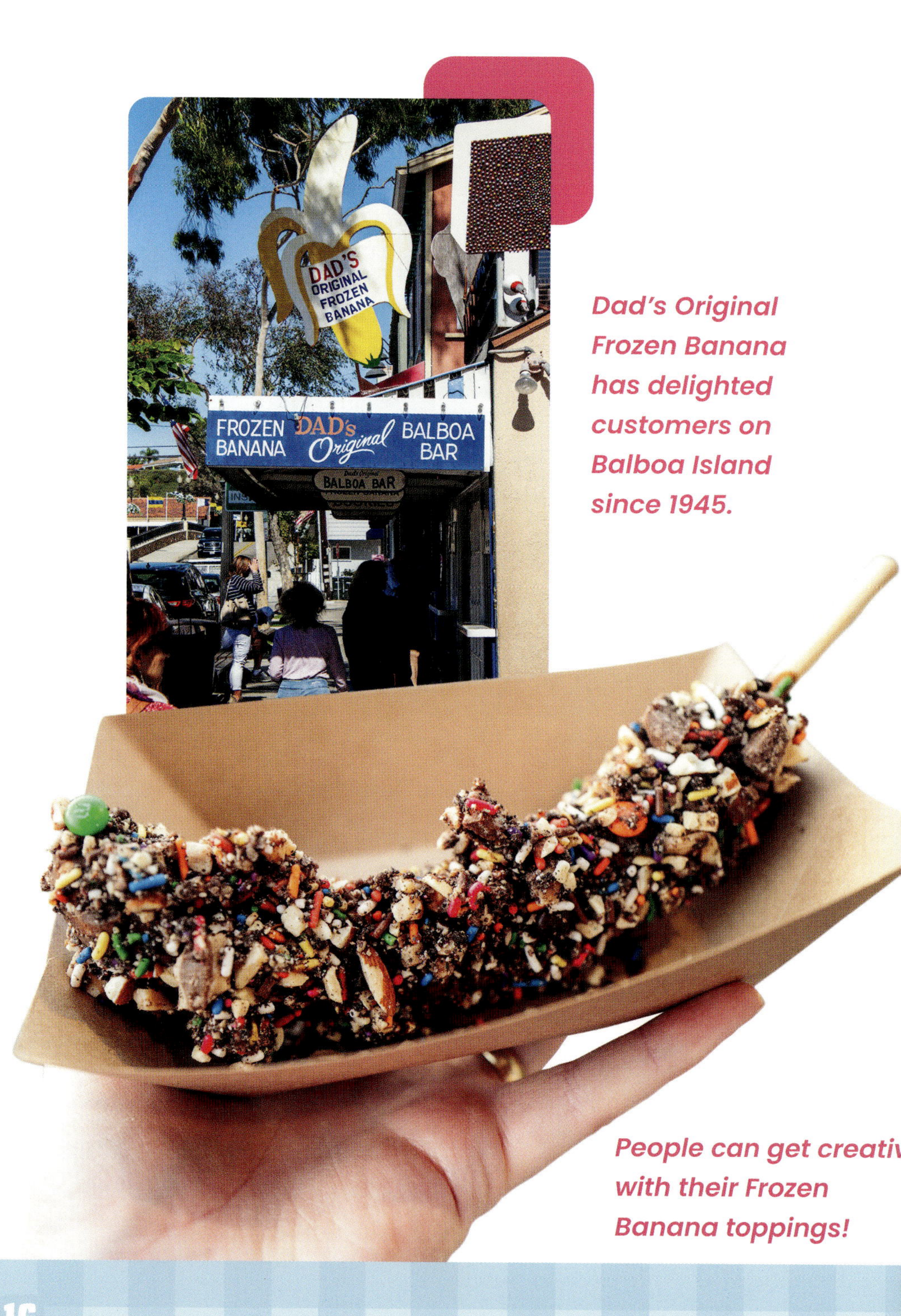

Dad's Original Frozen Banana has delighted customers on Balboa Island since 1945.

People can get creativ with their Frozen Banana toppings!

Balboa Island is in Newport Beach, California. The special community is known for its charming (yet expensive) homes, **mainstay** small businesses, and delicious food. One of Balboa Island's most famous foods is the Frozen Banana. This treat is made by freezing a banana on a stick and dipping it in chocolate or yogurt. Many people enjoy adding other toppings such as nuts and sprinkles.

An American classic, the Banana Split, is made using one banana cut in half lengthwise. Between the two slices sit three scoops of different ice cream flavors: vanilla, chocolate, and strawberry. It is then drizzled in a sweet sauce, often chocolate, and topped with cherries and whipped cream. It can also be sprinkled with nuts to add crunch!

The Banana Split can be traced back to 1904 in Latrobe, Pennsylvania. Then, a young **soda jerk** named David Strickler made what may have been the first Banana Split. It wasn't long before the dessert became a national favorite!

Some people enjoy
fresh strawberries on
their Banana Split.

Maple Taffy is a quick and easy treat to make.

Wintertime in Canada is long, cold, and snowy. The season is made a little bit sweeter with Maple Taffy! Traditionally, this simple treat is made by boiling maple sap to about 234 °F (112 °C).

The sweet, molten goodness is then poured onto clean snow.

The syrup cools slowly into a soft candy. It is picked up with a wooden stick and enjoyed right away!

Two children in Quebec use twigs to serve themselves Maple Taffy in the 1950s.

CHAPTER 4

FROZEN DESSERTS FROM ASIA AND THE PACIFIC

Kulfi (pronounced kuhl-fee) is a thick and creamy frozen dessert from India. Traditional flavors come from common Indian cuisine ingredients, including saffron, cardamom, and rose. The dessert originated in Delhi in the 16th century. It is made by slowly cooking sweetened,

COMPLETE AN ACTIVITY HERE!

In India, Kulfi is sold by street vendors known as kulfiwallahs.

flavored milk and other ingredients. The mixture is then poured into Kulfi molds and frozen solid.

Traditional Kakigōri is drizzled in green tea syrup and topped with red bean paste.

Japan's summers are hot and humid. The Japanese shaved ice treat called Kakigōri is the perfect thing to beat the heat. The first recorded instance of shaved ice as a dessert dates back 1,300 years. Today, many cafes throughout Japan serve Kakigōri.

The dessert is made by pouring flavored syrups over shaved ice. Common Kakigōri flavors include **matcha**, melon, and strawberry.

Condensed milk is a common Kakigōri topping.

DID YOU KNOW?

July 25 is Kakigōri Day in Japan. On this day in 1933, Japan experienced the highest national recorded temperature at the time.

I-Tim-Pad preparation is fun to watch!

I-Tim-Pad is a fun and unique way to enjoy dessert. This Thai treat is made by pouring an ice-cream mixture onto an extremely cold metal sheet. The mixture is chopped and spread thin until it is frozen solid. Other ingredients can be added at this stage. Then, the chef scrapes the ice cream into several thin rolls. The rolls are placed in a cup and can be topped with other fixings.

I-Tim-Pad is also called stir-fried ice cream or rolled ice cream.

MORE FROZEN DESSERTS FROM AROUND THE WORLD!

1. Paletas (Mexico)
2. Açaí na Tigela (Brazil)
3. Peppermint Crisp Fridge Tart (South Africa)
4. Booza (Syria)
5. Snow Ice (Taiwan)
6. Halo-Halo (Philippines)
7. Hokey Pokey (New Zealand)

Countries and cultures around the world have their own unique and traditional desserts. Their ingredients and techniques can be similar to or very different from one another.

MAKING CONNECTIONS

TEXT-TO-SELF

Do you like frozen desserts? If so, what is your favorite kind?

TEXT-TO-TEXT

Have you read any other books about food from around the world? What did you learn in those books that was not in this one?

TEXT-TO-WORLD

What are some other ways, besides dessert, that countries and cultures from around the world are special and different from one another?

GLOSSARY

churning — moving or stirring powerfully.

culture — the language, customs, ideas, and art of a particular group of people.

evaporate — to turn from liquid into gas.

mainstay — a key part of something.

matcha — a green powder made from ground green tea leaves.

milestone — an important event or turning point in history or in a person's life.

puree — a smooth, creamy substance made of crushed fruit or vegetables.

soda jerk — a person who served and sold soft drinks and ice cream at a soda fountain. Soda fountains were often located in drugstores, candy stores, and other businesses.

Turkish Empire — also known as the Ottoman Empire, an empire of the Turks that existed from about 1300 to 1918 and that at times included much of the land bordering the Mediterranean Sea.

INDEX

DiscoverRoo!
ONLINE RESOURCES

This book is filled with videos, puzzles, games, and more! Scan the QR codes* while you read, or visit the website below to make this book pop.

popbooksonline.com/frozen

*Scanning QR codes requires a web-enabled smart device with a QR code reader app and a camera.